Being a Good Parent

Elf-help for
Being a Good Parent

written by
Janet Geisz

illustrated by
R.W. Alley

ONE
CARING
PLACE
Abbey Press

Text © 2000 by Janet Geisz
Illustrations © 2000 by St. Meinrad Archabbey
Published by One Caring Place
Abbey Press
St. Meinrad, Indiana 47577

Library of Congress Catalog Number
00-90141

ISBN 0-87029-335-4

Printed in the United States of America

Foreword

Although parenting is one of the most crucial tasks any of us will ever undertake, there's no mandatory training for it, no required reading, no licensing or certification. It's probably fair to say that no one is ever fully prepared for the perils of parenting.

Yet it's also true that no one is ever prepared for the *rewards* of being a parent: the natural and pure love of a child, the delight of watching your child learn and grow and become.

This little guide to parenting suggests ways to enhance the joys of bringing up your child, while rising to the challenges. Written by a specialist in child development, it supports parents in the awesome responsibility of molding the development of another human being.

May the ideas presented here help you to raise a child with the emotional strength and spiritual fortitude to last a lifetime. And may you reap the ultimate reward of parenting—more love and joy than you ever knew your heart could hold.

1.

Generously express the love
you feel for your child in all you
say and do. Children thrive on
love. They can never receive
too much.

2.

A child's thinking is shaped by experience. To experience love, a child needs to feel hugs and kisses, to hear caring words, to see acts of kindness.

3.

Every child is a blessing and needs to know this. If you have more than one child, honor their differences and affirm the special qualities each brings to the family. You can deter sibling rivalry by treating them with equal love and respect.

4.

Parenting is a privilege and your most important responsibility. Make it a top priority in your life. Be involved in your children's school, sports, and activities. Giving your children time and attention shows how much you value them.

5.

Children imitate what adults do, not what they say. Model the kind of morals and behavior you expect from your child.

6.

Know your child well by listening to her—her hopes, dreams, fears, and desires. Listening attentively honors and validates who she is. Be careful not to rush in with unsolicited judgments, advice, or solutions. Simply listen.

Ella
Elf History
Quiz

7.

Allow your child to express her feelings—joy, excitement, sadness, fear, disappointment, and anger. Feelings are neither "good" nor "bad." By talking with your child about her feelings, you can help her learn to handle them wisely and solve problems constructively.

8.

Respect for authority begins with respect for one's parents. Children respect adults they can trust. Earn your child's respect by being fair and reliable.

9.

Honesty is essential for a trusting relationship. Aside from joyful childhood fantasies, like the Tooth Fairy and Santa (which are worth the pretense), be honest with your child. It will teach him to be honest with you.

10.

Children learn how to treat other people by observing how their parents treat each other. Showing respect for your child's other parent is one of the ways you can teach your child to treat people with dignity.

11.

Children develop new skills through trial and error. Be patient and encouraging as your child tries to learn. And be assured there will be messes to clean up!

12.

Expose your child to a rich variety of experiences, adventures, and activities. Share your own passions and hobbies with him. Allow him to explore new interests. These experiences provide background knowledge for all future learning.

13.

Play is the "business" of children—their primary activity for learning and development. Play enhances physical, social, and emotional growth, while building thinking skills. Give your child ample opportunities to play, and be there to play with her often.

14.

Make sure your child has enough unstructured time—time just to be a kid. Kids need a break from lessons, sports, and other formal activities. Too much pressure to perform and achieve can lead to burnout or underachievement.

15.

Imagining is one of childhood's most beautiful and natural pleasures. Stimulate your child's imagination by providing time away from technology for him to use his own mind. A child with nothing to do will employ his imagination to create new ideas and exciting adventures.

16.

Celebrate with your child often—special days, faith traditions, victories, courageous efforts. Celebrations establish family rituals and memories that bond meaningful relationships. Celebrations lighten the soul and bring fun to life!

17.

Share your spiritual beliefs with your child. Talk about times when you have experienced the power of prayer, or when your faith has brought you hope and comfort. Help your child to feel a part of your religious traditions and your spiritual community.

18.

Explore the beauty and bounty of nature with your child. Appreciate the wonders of the world with him. Reponsible caring for nature begins with childhood experiences—like walking in the woods, feeling the spray of a waterfall, or dangling feet in a mountain stream.

19.

Enjoy reading with your child every day. Reading lovingly and patiently will foster closeness, increase your child's chance of school success, and promote a lifelong love of learning.

20.

Allow your child to gain independence as he becomes more and more capable of handling the responsibility. Expressing your belief in his abilities will give him the confidence to pursue new challenges and accomplish new feats. His successes, in turn, will boost his self-esteem.

21.

Let your child make choices. Children learn responsibility and judgment when they experience the natural rewards and consequences of their own choices.

22.

Allow your child to fail at times. Surviving failure builds up confidence to take chances and try new things. Overcoming failure helps teach the connection between effort and success.

23.

Strive for "balanced parenting"—neither too controlling nor too permissive. When parents are too authoritarian, children miss opportunities to learn self-control; they may try to gain control through defiance, self-destruction, or withdrawal. When parents are too permissive, children don't learn to earn privileges or to delay gratification.

24.

Recognize the difference between childhood needs and wants— and learn to say no. Children want many more things than they need. Help your child learn how to do without, or work toward and earn, the things she wants.

25.

Guide and support your child by setting carefully selected limits. Your child will learn self-discipline by observing these limits— and accountability when he challenges them.

26.

<u>Positive</u> discipline allows your child to experience the consequences of poor choices. <u>Punitive</u> discipline (physical or emotional) proves adult power but turns a child's thoughts to anger. Lovingly use positive discipline, and your child will learn from his mistakes through reflective reasoning.

27.

Insist that your child do
her share of the chores.
Age-appropriate chores help
children become industrious
and responsible. Teamwork
promotes reliability and
confidence within the family.

28.

Mutual respect fosters an enduring parent-child relationship. Respect your child by accepting him for being the wonderful person he is. Whatever his temperament or rate of development, he is abundantly gifted with unlimited potential. Honor your child's potential.

29.

Remember, <u>you</u> are the expert on your child. If someone questions your child's potential, share what you know about his attributes. Work together to build upon his talents, strengths, and abilities.

30.

Know your child and be alert to signs of too much stress. Life can sometimes be traumatic, but if you catch emotional difficulties early, you have a better chance of helping your child through the rough times.

31.

Let your child know you are
on her side. Be her advocate
when she needs adult support.
Resist rescuing her, however,
when she is capable of handling
the problem on her own.
Finding out she can handle
her own difficulties builds
self-esteem.

32.

Vulnerability is a fact of childhood. Parents have the responsibility to shelter a child's innocence and trust. Protect your child from abusive language or behavior by family members, acquaintances, or the media.

33.

Take good care of yourself.
You will enjoy parenting more
if you are healthy, rested, happy,
and at peace. Healthy living
teaches your child how to take
care of herself—body and soul.

34.

Become informed about the natural stages of child development. It's easier to deal with a difficult stage if you know what's normal and what to expect. Realizing that all children go through predictable, challenging behaviors will help you to relax and enjoy your child at every age and stage.

35.

Being a loving and effective parent is a complex job for which we receive no formal training. When you need support, seek help from an experienced relative, spiritual leader, child development specialist, or family counselor. Consult parenting books or consider joining a parent support group.

36.

Family is the most significant influence in a child's life. Family is the setting in which your child learns how to respectfully interact with others, how to love and be loved. Protect and cherish your family as a nurturing and supportive haven for your child.

37.

Value these precious childhood years. Children are not about achievements, grades, test scores, or trophies. Children are about innocence, discovery, enthusiasm, and laughter. Let your child enjoy being a kid, without having to prove himself or perform for others.

38.

God has granted you the privilege and responsibility of being a parent. The everyday love you give your child will determine the value of this experience. Cherish your child and this extraordinary opportunity!

Janet Geisz is a child development specialist working with vulnerable and troubled children. She has been an educator for thirty years and a parent for twenty-five years. Holding an M.A. degree in the education of children with emotional and behavioral disorders, she is currently in a doctoral program studying early childhood development and learning.

Illustrator for the Abbey Press Elf-help Books, **R.W. Alley** also illustrates and writes children's books. He lives in Barrington, Rhode Island, with his wife, daughter, and son.

The Story of the Abbey Press Elves

The engaging figures that populate the Abbey Press "elf-help" line of publications and products first appeared in 1987 on the pages of a small self-help book called *Be-good-to-yourself Therapy*. Shaped by the publishing staff's vision and defined in R.W. Alley's inventive illustrations, they lived out author Cherry Hartman's gentle, self-nurturing advice with charm, poignancy, and humor.

Reader response was so enthusiastic that more Elf-help Books were soon under way, a still-growing series that has inspired a line of related gift products.

The especially endearing character featured in the early books—sporting a cap with a mood-changing candle in its peak—has since been joined by a spirited female elf with flowers in her hair.

These two exuberant, sensitive, resourceful, kindhearted, lovable sprites, along with their lively elfin community, reveal what's truly important as they offer messages of joy and wonder, playfulness and co-creation, wholeness and serenity, the miracle of life and the mystery of God's love.

With wisdom and whimsy, these little creatures with long noses demonstrate the elf-help way to a rich and fulfilling life.

Elf-help Books

Elf-help for Being a Good Parent
#20103 $4.95   ISBN 0-87029-335-4

Gratitude Therapy
#20105 $4.95   ISBN 0-87029-332-X

Garden Therapy
#20116 $4.95   ISBN 0-87029-325-7

Elf-help for Busy Moms
#20117 $4.95   ISBN 0-87029-324-9

Trust-in-God Therapy
#20119 $4.95   ISBN 0-87029-322-2

Elf-help for Overcoming Depression
#20134 $4.95   ISBN 0-87029-315-X

New Baby Therapy
#20140 $4.95   ISBN 0-87029-307-9

Grief Therapy for Men
#20141 $4.95   ISBN 0-87029-306-0

Living From Your Soul
#20146 $4.95   ISBN 0-87029-303-6

Teacher Therapy
#20145 $4.95   ISBN 0-87029-302-8

Be-good-to-your-family Therapy
#20154 $4.95   ISBN 0-87029-300-1

Stress Therapy
#20153 $4.95   ISBN 0-87029-301-X

Making-sense-out-of-suffering Therapy
#20156 $4.95   ISBN 0-87029-296-X

Get Well Therapy
#20157 $4.95   ISBN 0-87029-297-8

Anger Therapy
#20127 $4.95   ISBN 0-87029-292-7

Caregiver Therapy
#20164 $4.95   ISBN 0-87029-285-4

Self-esteem Therapy
#20165 $4.95   ISBN 0-87029-280-3

Take-charge-of-your-life Therapy
#20168 $4.95   ISBN 0-87029-271-4

Work Therapy
#20166 $4.95   ISBN 0-87029-276-5

Everyday-courage Therapy
#20167 $4.95   ISBN 0-87029-274-9

Peace Therapy
#20176 $4.95   ISBN 0-87029-273-0

Friendship Therapy
#20174 $4.95   ISBN 0-87029-270-6

Christmas Therapy (color edition)
#20175 $5.95   ISBN 0-87029-268-4

Grief Therapy
#20178 $4.95   ISBN 0-87029-267-6

Happy Birthday Therapy
#20181 $4.95   ISBN 0-87029-260-9

Forgiveness Therapy
#20184 $4.95   ISBN 0-87029-258-7

Keep-life-simple Therapy
#20185 $4.95   ISBN 0-87029-257-9

Celebrate-your-womanhood Therapy
#20189 $4.95   ISBN 0-87029-254-4

Acceptance Therapy (color edition)
#20182 $5.95   ISBN 0-87029-259-5

Acceptance Therapy
#20190 $4.95   ISBN 0-87029-245-5

Keeping-up-your-spirits Therapy
#20195 $4.95   ISBN 0-87029-242-0

Play Therapy
#20200 $4.95   ISBN 0-87029-233-1

Slow-down Therapy
#20203 $4.95   ISBN 0-87029-229-3

One-day-at-a-time Therapy
#20204 $4.95   ISBN 0-87029-228-5

Prayer Therapy
#20206 $4.95   ISBN 0-87029-225-0

Be-good-to-your-marriage Therapy
#20205 $4.95   ISBN 0-87029-224-2

Be-good-to-yourself Therapy (hardcover)
#20196 $10.95   ISBN 0-87029-243-9

Be-good-to-yourself Therapy
#20255 $4.95   ISBN 0-87029-209-9

Available at your favorite giftshop or bookstore—
or directly from One Caring Place, Abbey Press
Publications, St. Meinrad, IN 47577.
Or call 1-800-325-2511.